My First
GEOMETRIC
DESIGNS
Coloring Book

Anna Pomaska

Dover Publications
Garden City, New York

D1412267

Note

Learn about shapes and practice your counting skills with this book full of geometric designs. There are 13 different shapes featured including some that you probably are familiar with like the circle, square, star, heart, and triangle. Other shapes are not as common and you might need some help to figure them out like the octagon, pentagon, and hexagon, so we have included a small picture of the shape next to the word in the caption to help you. Each page has a question about the different shapes plus an answer, which you will see printed upside down at the bottom. After you answer the questions, have fun coloring the pages!

Copyright

Copyright © 2010 by Dover Publications
All rights reserved.

Bibliographical Note

My First Geometric Designs Coloring Book is a new work, first published by
Dover Publications in 2010.

International Standard Book Number

ISBN-13: 978-0-486-47557-8
ISBN-10: 0-486-47557-3

Manufactured in the United States of America
47557307   2023
www.doverpublications.com

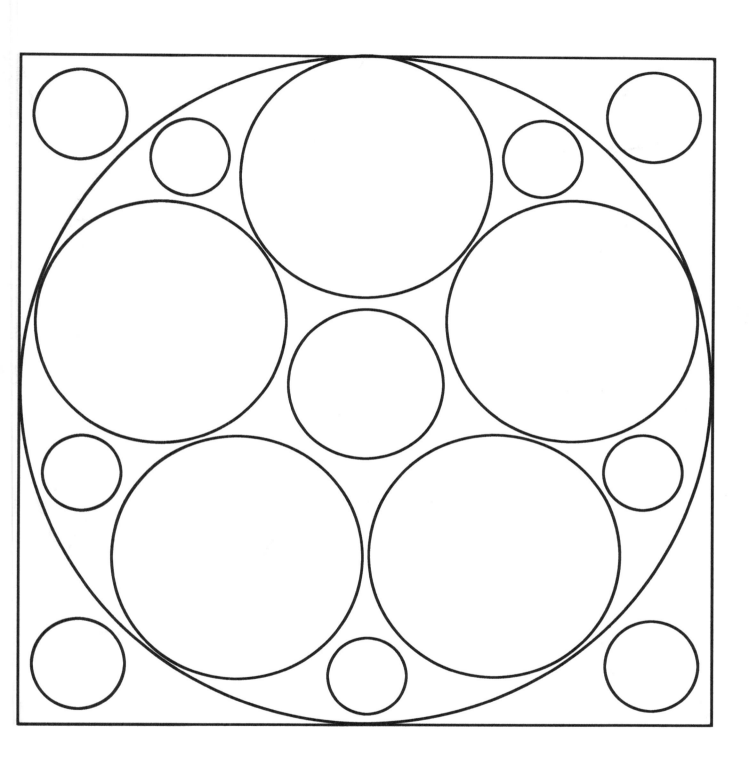

Look at all these circles ◯! See if you can count them all.
Don't forget to include the large circle!

How many diamonds ◇ are mixed in with the circles ◯?
How many circles do you count?

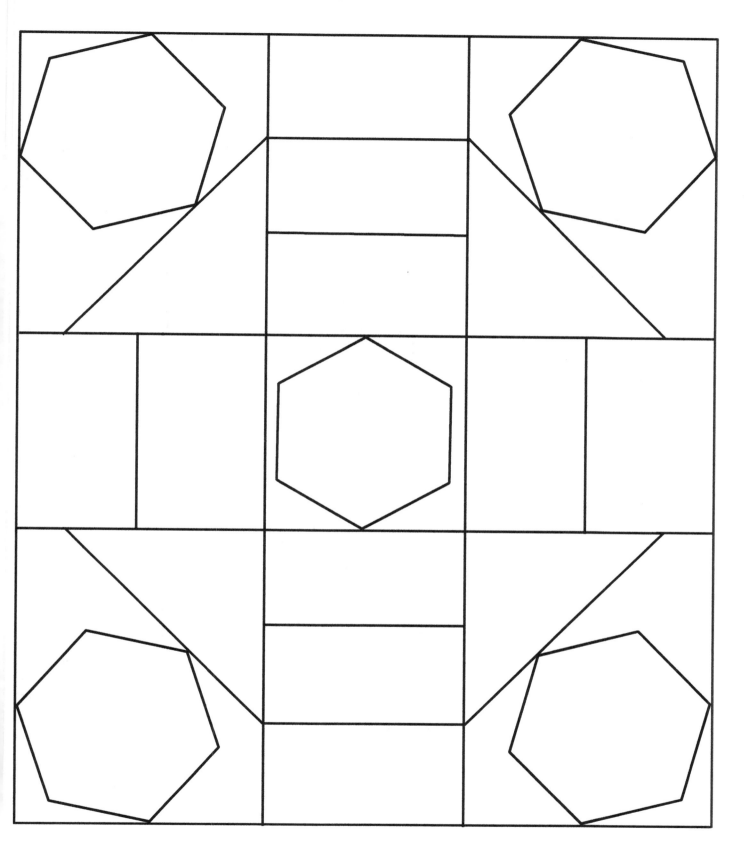

There are hexagons ⬡, triangles △, and rectangles ▯ in this design.
See if you can find them all.

Here you will notice that not all triangles △ look the same. As long as they have
3 sides they are triangles! How many do you count?

4

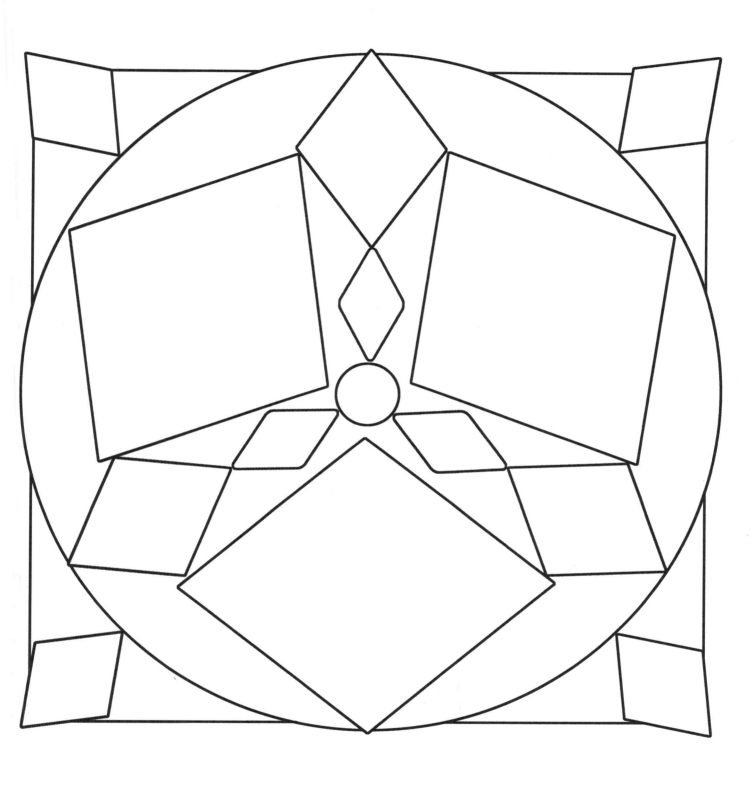

How many diamonds ◇ do you see? There are also some circles ◯.
Count the circles.

5

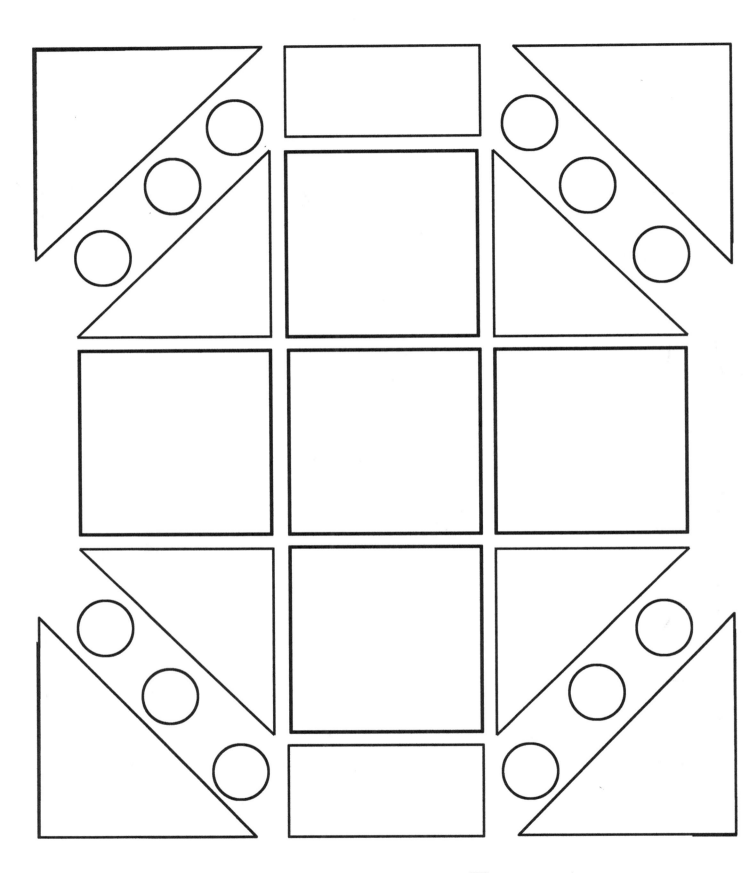

There are 4 different shapes in this design: Squares ☐, triangles △, circles ◯, and rectangles ☐. How many do you count?

Answer: 5 squares, 8 triangles, 12 circles, 2 rectangles

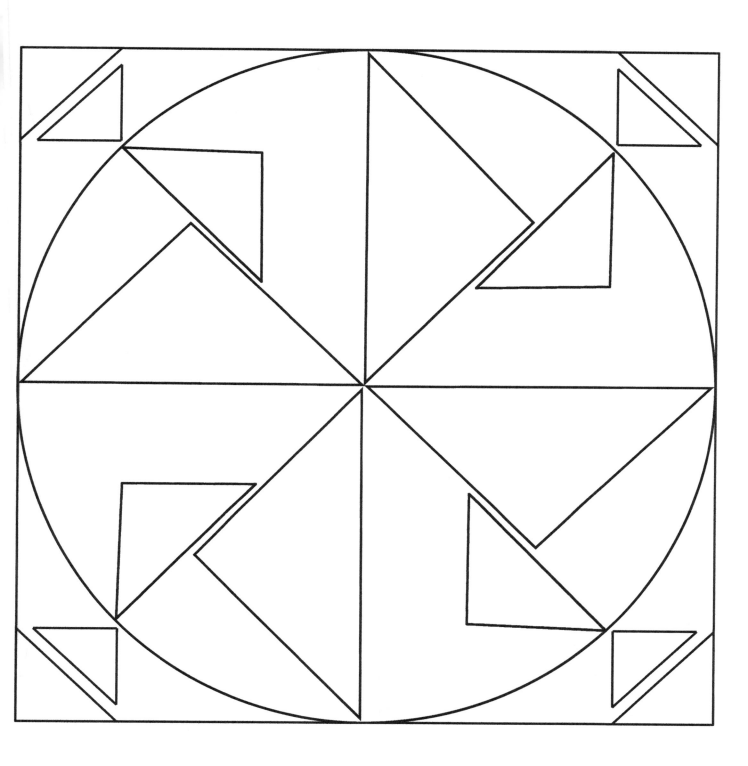

This one is a little tricky. Go slowly and see if you can find all of the triangles △.

Hexagons ⬡ have six sides and these stars ☆ have five points.
How many can you find?

Answer: 14 hexagons, 2 stars

This design is full of triangles △ and hearts ♡. Count them all.

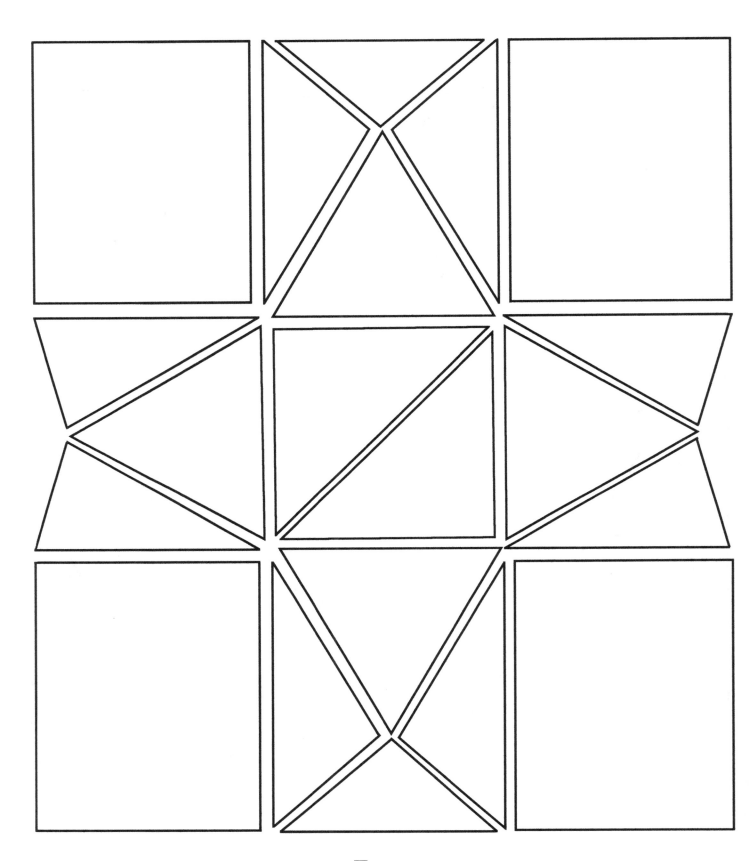

Count all the rectangles ▯ and triangles △ in this design.

Answer: 4 rectangles, 16 triangles

This star is surrounded by diamonds ◇ and squares ▢. How many do you see?
Remember, diamonds have 2 pointed ends.

Large triangles △ and big and small circles ◯ make up this design.
See if you can find them all.

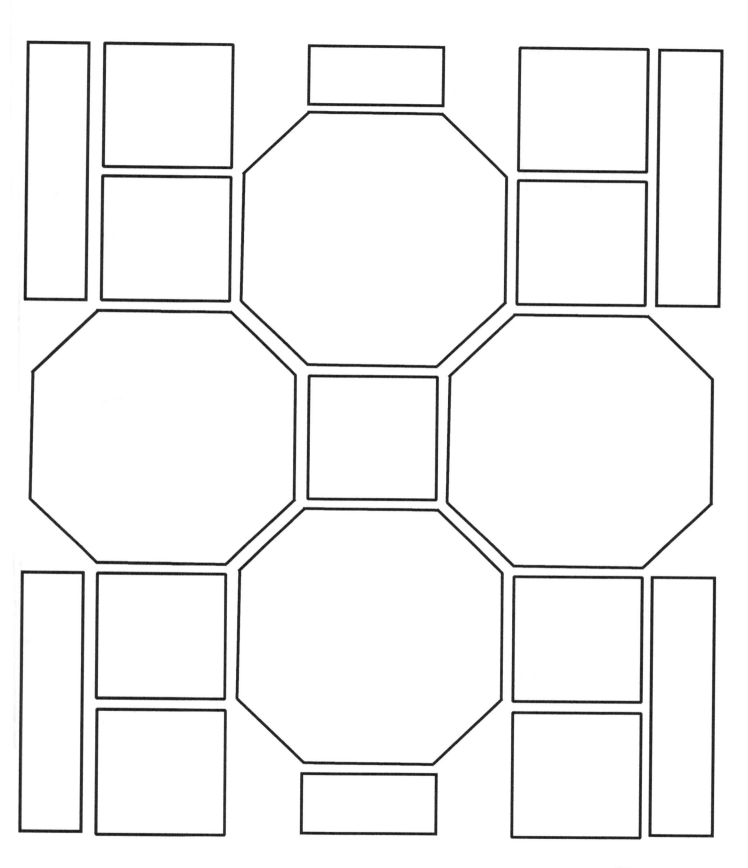

There are **3** different shapes in this design. Can you find all the rectangles ▯,
squares ☐, and octagons ⬡ ?

In this design there are 2 different types of stars ☆ and some diamonds ◇.
Count all of the stars together and count the diamonds.

Look closely at this design and you'll see a star formed by triangles △ and a pentagon ⬠. How many triangles and pentagons do you see?

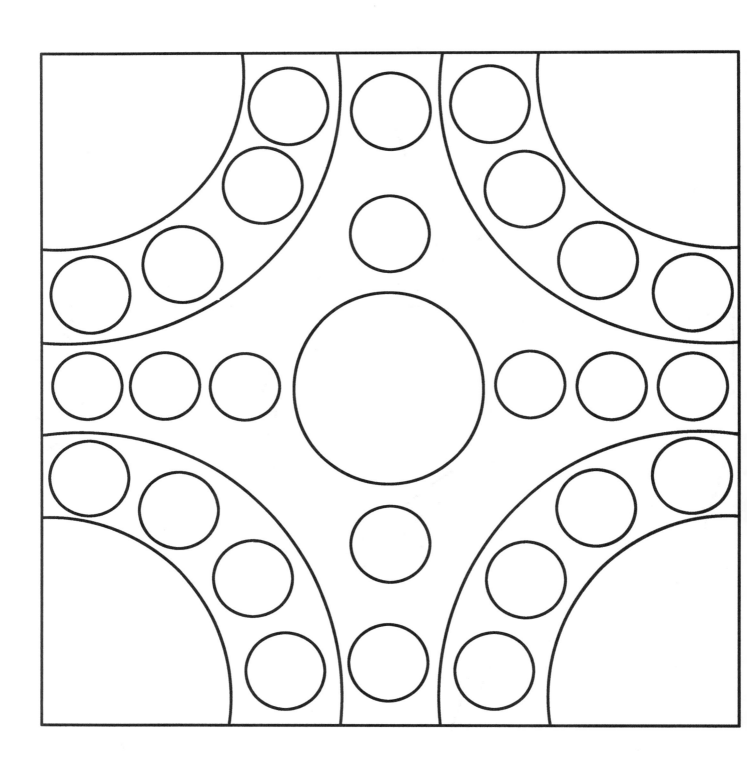

These circles ◯ look like bubbles. Count all the circles.
Don't forget to count the large circle.

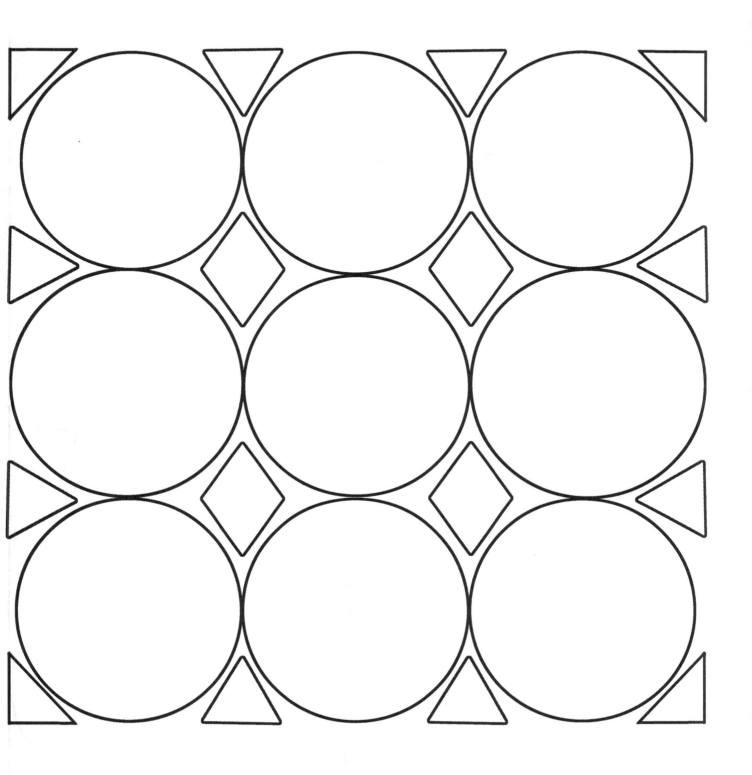

This pattern has triangles △ , circles ◯ , and diamonds ◇ .
Remember diamonds have 4 sides and triangles have 3.

These crescents ☾ look like moons among the stars ☆.
Count all the crescents and stars.

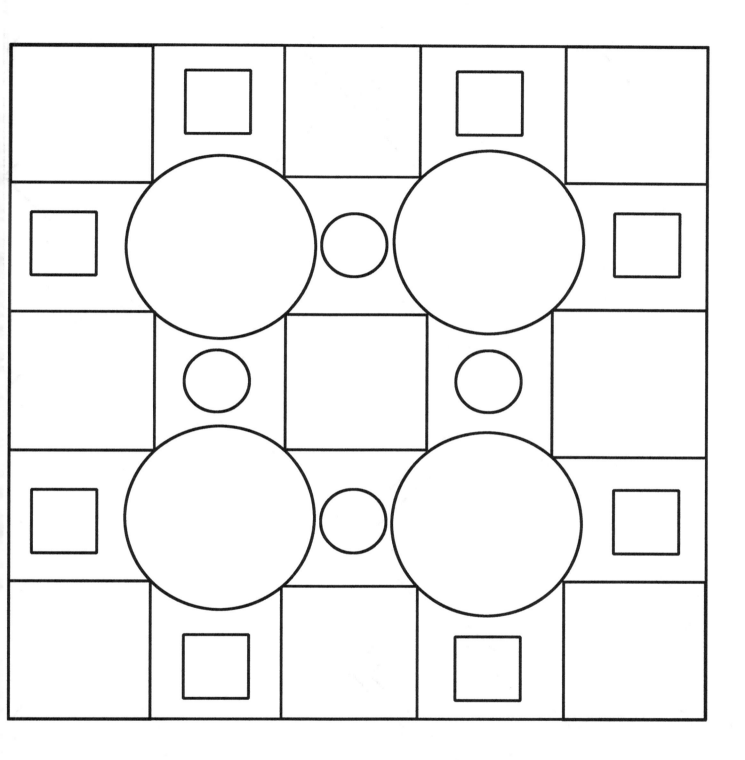

Here are big and small circles ◯ and squares ☐. How many do you see?

Diamonds ◇ and rectangles ▢ both have 4 sides. How many can you find?

Answer: 11 diamonds, 8 rectangles

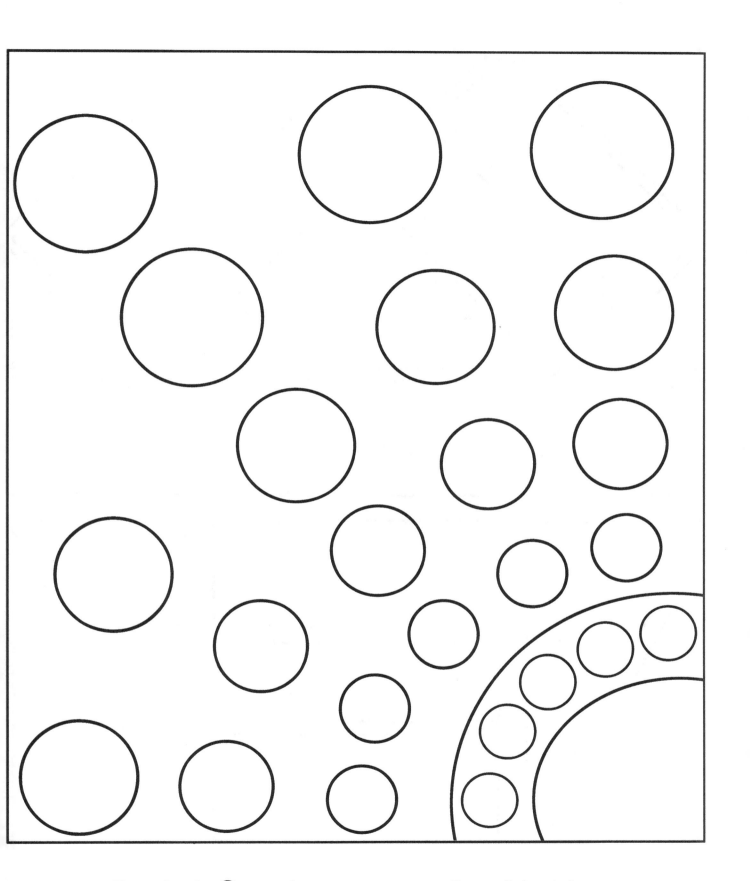

Tons of circles ◯ are in this geometric pattern. Count all the circles.

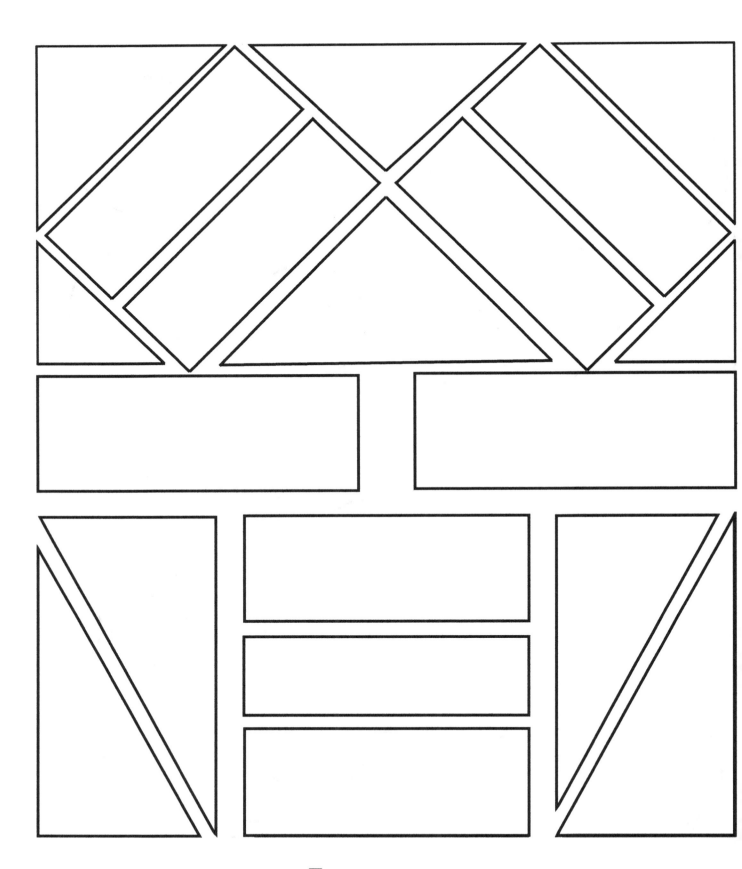

How many rectangles ▢ and triangles △ do you see in this design?
Remember, triangles must have 3 sides, but don't have to look the same.

Ovals ⬭ look like squashed circles ◯ . How many ovals are in this design?

This should be easy! Hexagons  have 6 sides and ovals  have none.
Find the hexagons and ovals.

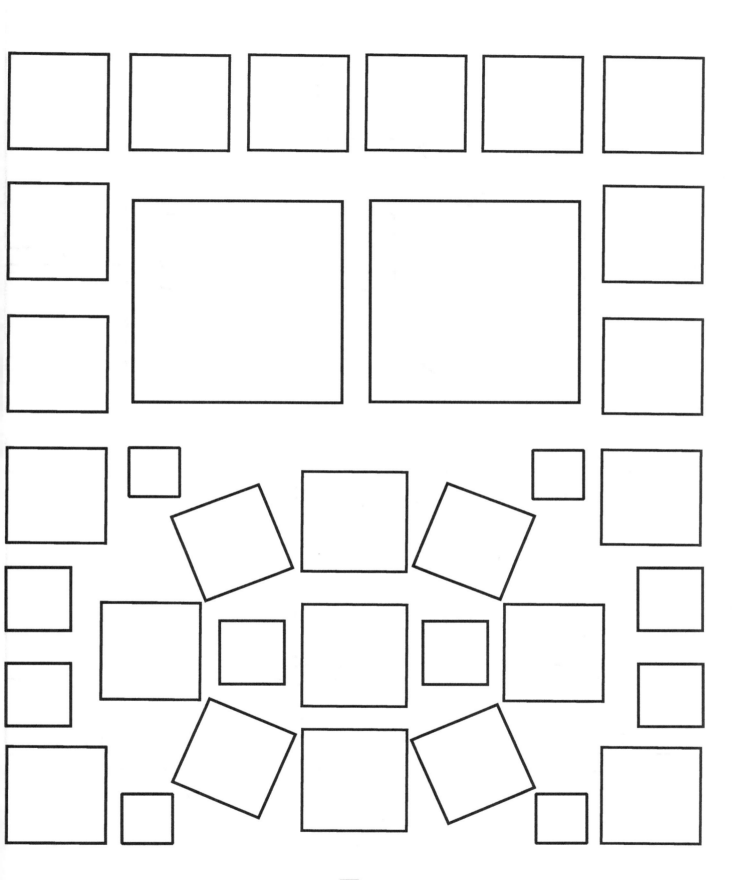

Three different sizes of squares ▢ make up this geometric pattern.
Count all the squares.

25

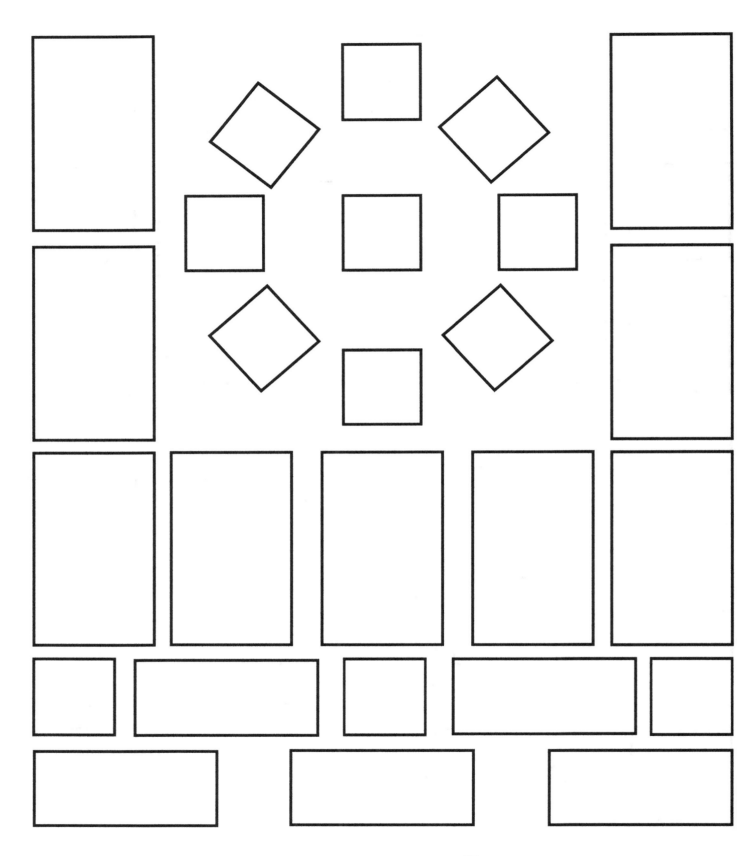

Count all the squares ▢ and rectangles ▯ in this design.

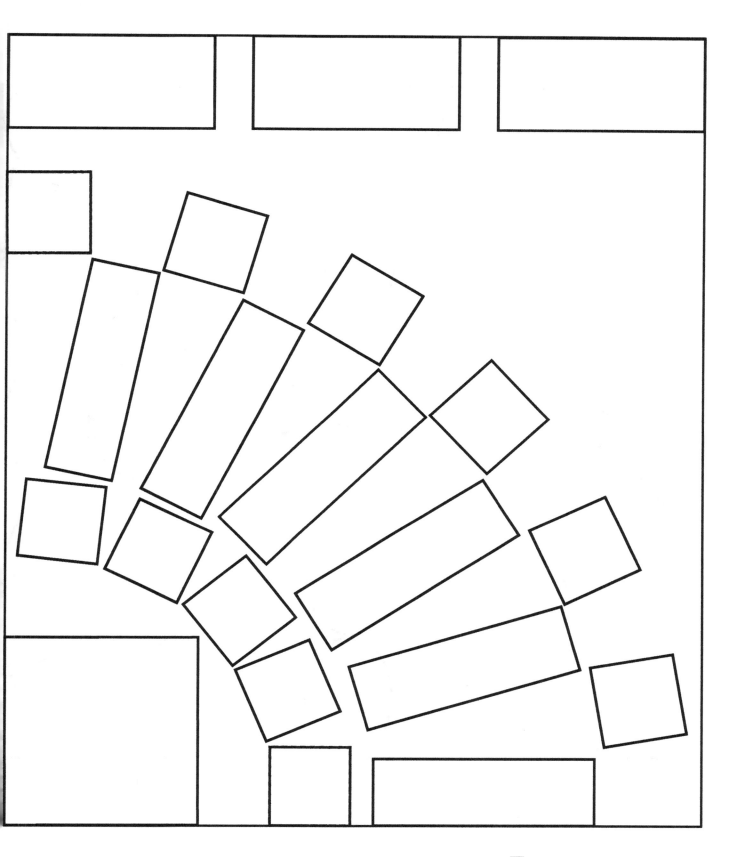

This design looks like a sunset using squares ☐ and rectangles ☐. Count all the shapes then color the picture to look like a sunset.

Hearts ♡ and ovals ◯ don't have any sides to count. Hearts do **have a**
pointed end; ovals don't. Have fun coloring and counting the **shapes.**

Triangles △ and crescents ℂ are all mixed together in this design.
Find them all and count them.

These crescents C and ovals ◯ make a pretty design. How many do you see?

30

Answer: 8 crescents, 13 ovals